Thorpe Hamlet Street Names

by Thorpe Hamlet History Group

Second edition 2016

Occasional paper 1

Published by Thorpe Hamlet History Group

Copyright Thorpe Hamlet History Group 2016

Map uses Ordnance Survey OpenData : Crown Copyright and database right 2010

First published 2009

Second edition 2016

ISBN 978-0-9955487-0-1

Printed by Colman Print, Norwich

Thorpe Hamlet History Group

Information about the Thorpe Hamlet History Group is at www.thorpehamlet.org.uk

The Group may be contacted via enquiries@thorpehamlet.org.uk or by telephoning 01603 436149. The Group will welcome any further information about Thorpe Hamlet street names, past or present.

The Group's other publications are:

A Thorpe Hamlet Miscellany (2016), a collection of over 100 articles about Thorpe Hamlet by June Marriage for the St. Matthew's Church parish magazine

Thorpe Hamlet Shops Then and Now (second edition 2016), Occasional Paper 2

INTRODUCTION

Our names give us a personal sense of being. They are given to us by our parents, and are used by our family, friends and colleagues and teachers throughout our lives. Our name is our own, even if we sometimes adapt it or change part of it when getting married.

And so it is for the places where we live and have our homes. Our address is on our passports; the postie knows where to deliver our letters, and we use it when filling in forms, but we often have no idea of where the names of our streets, avenues, lanes or closes come from. It was with this in mind that the Thorpe Hamlet History Group began its research into the naming of streets. It has led us into the history of Thorpe Hamlet, foreign parts, military heritage and the personal history of the people of Norwich. It has also led us up many blind alleys, and, as you will see, in some cases left us defeated. We hope to fill in the gaps in our knowledge, so this is an on-going project. We would be pleased for any help you may have in helping us to complete our project. Details of how to contact the Group are on the reverse of the title page.

Acknowledgements

As you can see from the above introduction, the production of this paper was not a simple task; members of the Group are therefore very grateful to all the people, and organisations for the help which they made readily available to us. Over the lengthy period of research we received many snippets of information, and comments.

What is a street?

For our second occasional paper, on shops, we had to decide what constituted a shop. Streets might seem simpler to define, but it is not necessarily so. Our aim has been to include those streets which have their own postal address rather than including the name of another street in the address. On that basis a number of residential blocks that are named as 'courts' are excluded. But it doesn't mean that all the streets we have included have been adopted, in the sense of being maintained by the Norfolk County Council, as highway authority. Nor do they all have street name signs, or ones that can easily be read.

If you think we have committed sins of commission or omission please let us know.

The streets we have included are detailed, with the origin of their names, from page 3 onwards. They are listed on page 16 with links to the grid on the map.

THE STREET NAMES OF THORPE HAMLET

- A -

Albert Place

Named after Prince Albert, son of the Duke of Saxe-Coburg-Gotha, the husband of Queen Victoria. He died of typhoid on 14th December 1861.

Albion Way

This road was named by public vote. The wherry 'Albion', built in Suffolk, sailed the river as a trading wherry, but is now a pleasure wherry which may be hired.

Wherry 'Albion'

Aldryche Road

The Aldryche family served Norwich well in the 15th and 16th centuries. Thomas, a draper by trade, was sheriff in 1497 and Mayor in 1507 and 1516. His son Thomas also served as Mayor and in Parliament. He lived in the flint house in Colegate, which was once the Labour Exchange, and is now an office-suite, St. Clement's House.

Aspland Road

Named after a large mansion in this area called Aspland House, which was owned by Robert Aspland Cooper, a wholesale confectioner. The grounds extended from St. Matthew's Road to Thorpe Road.

- B -

Barrack Road

Named after the adjacent Britannia Barracks, now a prison, to which it leads.

Barton Way

No information available. It serves the City Office Park, off Carrow Road.

Beatrice Road

Beatrice was a daughter of the developer Isaac Bugg Coaks. This road was one of the six 'Lady' roads. See also Ella, Ethel, Florence, Marion and Primrose Roads.

Beatrice Road

Belsize Road

The name probably comes from Belasis, a Norman French name meaning Bell Assize or beautiful seat or place.

Bertram Way

This development was built on the site of the former Bertram Books warehouse. See also The Nest for a reference to an earlier incarnation of the site.

Bishop Bridge Road

Named after the distinctive bridge over the River Wensum, which was built in 1340 and once had a fortified Gate House. For hundreds of years it was the last bridge before the sea at Great Yarmouth.

Borrowdale Drive

Two possible alternatives (neither confirmed). Firstly, a reference to the Lakeland beauty spot, the second to honour George Borrow.

Britannia Road

Roman name for Ancient Britain given to Britannia Barracks built in 1887, with the request from the City Council that the building should have a pleasing appearance! Road adopted in 1910. Britannia was the Regimental Badge of the Norfolk Regiment. In the Peninsula Wars the Portuguese thought the badge was the Virgin Mary. This led to the Norfolk Regiment being nicknamed 'The Holy Boys'. Britannia Road runs both north and south of Plumstead Road, but has the same name on both sides.

Britannia Barracks, now home to HMP Norwich and Café Britannia

Broadsman Close

Named after the steam train - a regular service from Norwich to London - as it adjoins the railway lines running into Thorpe station.

- C -

Camp Grove

The area where the rebel Robert Kett was said to have set up his camp. It was here that Dr Matthew Parker, later the Archbishop of Canterbury and remembered today as 'Nosey Parker', addressed Kett and his men. The name also recalls Camp Road, which ran north-south through the area, parallel to St. Leonard's Road, prior to redevelopment in the late 1960s.

Canary Way

Named after Norwich City Football Club, popularly known as 'The Canaries' from 1907. The habit of weavers to keep canaries in their weaving lofts for company is said to have been brought over by the 'Strangers'.

The former Camp Road Photo: Michael Everitt

Carrow Road

The road from Carrow Abbey, a Benedictine Nunnery, founded in 1136. The line of this road has changed. From the junction of King Street and Carrow Hill a road can still be seen running down to the river. Here there used to be a bridge, with the road continuing to the east of what is now the football ground. But in the 1930s the present Carrow Bridge was built to the west. Now Koblenz Avenue and Canary Way take the main traffic, and Carrow Road hugs the football ground before rejoining its old route up to Thorpe Road. Worldwide, Carrow Road is likely to be the best-known street name in Thorpe Hamlet because it has given its name to the football club's ground.

Cedar Road

The author Kenneth Beckett in his book 'The Love of Trees' refers to the cedar as a picturesque tree giving a serenity to its planting area.

Chalk Hill Road

This road name means exactly what it says - a road on a chalk hill. The chalk from these workings were used in the building of Norwich Cathedral. It was the original name of Rosary Road before the housing between Rosary Road and Riverside Road was developed.

Cintra Road

Named after the treaty of Sintra in 1808 - Sir Arthur Wellesley engaged the French in Portugal early in the war. The engagement was a success and the French sued for an armistice.
See also Wellesley Avenue.

Clarence Road

The meadow between Thorpe Road and Carrow was to have been docks in a grandiose scheme of the early 19th century. In anticipation the road was named after the sailor prince, subsequently William IV.

Clarence Road

Cotman Road

Named after John Sell Cotman, prominent member of the Norwich School of Painters. In 1807 he set up an academy with lessons at £1 1s for four lessons. The road was re-named by Isaac Bugg Coaks. It was formerly called Grove Road, from the Grove House Estate.

Cozens Road

See also Hardy Road, both probably named after the Cozens-Hardy family.

Cremorne Lane

In 1868 the Cremorne Gardens and Gymnasium were set up by a Mr Walter Hart and presented a popular amenity at the time.

Croftholme Way

After 'Croft' and 'Holme', literally a piece of enclosed (arable land) often submerged in time of flood forming a small islet.

Cubitt Road

Possibly named after William Cubitt, a Norfolk-born engineer who was engaged to draw up plans to dredge the river Yare, to enable sea-going vessels to reach the city of Norwich.

- D -

Dugard Avenue

No information available.

- E -

Eden Close

Thought to be named after Anthony Eden (1897 - 1977), British Foreign Secretary and later Prime Minister in the year the close was constructed. He married Winston Churchill's niece.

Ella Road

Ella was a daughter of the developer Isaac Bugg Coaks. This road was one of the six 'Lady' roads. See also Beatrice, Ethel, Florence, Marion and Primrose Roads.

Ethel Road

Ethel was a daughter of the developer Isaac Bugg Coaks. This road was one of the six 'Lady' roads. See also Beatrice, Ella, Florence, Marion and Primrose Roads.

- F -

Fallowfield Close

Fallowfield was spoken of as early as 1317, and refers to the 'fallowing' of land for its recuperation.

Fernhill Lane

From the house built by Isaac Bugg Coaks, solicitor in the 1860s. When he died in 1909 the house remained empty until it was used as a military convalescent home. In 1927 it became a hotel. In World War II it was used for storing furniture from bomb damaged houses. It was demolished in 1959. See also Beatrice, Cotman, Ella, Ethel, Florence, Marion and Primrose Roads.

Ferry Road

Site of a ferry across the Wensum from Pull's Ferry and used by football supporters en route to 'The Nest' on Rosary Road.

Firwood Close

Stands on land once covered by fir woods which were felled for development purposes.

Florence Road

Florence was a daughter of the developer Isaac Bugg Coaks. This road was one of the six 'Lady' roads. See also Beatrice, Ella, Ethel, Florence and Primrose Roads.

Pull's Ferry, across the river from Ferry Road

- G -

Gas Hill

This was once the pathway to St Leonard's Priory. On old maps it is shown as the Pilgrims' Way. In May 1830 the Norwich Gas Company bought five acres of land to erect the gas works to supply the whole city, and the road became known as Gas House Hill, later Gas Hill. It is the steepest hill in Norwich, if not the whole of Norfolk, and is the location for the Gas Hill Gasp cycle race, revived in recent years, and now staged as part of the Lord Mayor's Festival in July.

The Gas Hill Gasp in the 1980s

Geoffrey Watling Way

Runs along the south side of the football ground, and is named in honour of a long-time chairman of Norwich City Football Club.

Gerald Close

No information available.

Glendenning Road

Major Glendenning DSO was manager of Laurence Scott Electromotors from 1921 - 1939. Glendenning Road is part of the Thorpe Park estate, built on the site of a former Laurence Scott factory. See also Scott and Wilson Roads.

Gravelfield Close

This area gave the citizens of Pockthorpe special rights of turf cutting, extracting gravel etc, - this close now occupies the site.

Guelph Road

A royal name emanating from a princely family in Germany. The present royal family is descended from the Guelphs through the House of Brunswick. Previously named Victoria Road.

Gurney Road

Named after John Gurney of Gurney's Bank, later Barclays, for his work in the preservation of Mousehold Heath. As Mayor, he officially declared the Heath open as a recreation area for the city on 12th May 1886.

- H -

Harbour Road

In the early years of the 20th century a Mr W. Botterill proposed a daring scheme for an inland naval base. 'Norwich a Port' was a popular slogan for this unfulfilled project and Harbour Road was so named in participation.

Hardy Road

See also Cozens Road, both probably named after the Cozens-Hardy family.

Harvey Lane

John Harvey acquired Thorpe Lodge (now Broadland District Council's offcies) in the early 18th century. To enlarge the grounds he changed the line of the road, which accounts for the bend at the Thorpe end, where Harvey Lane no longer follows the city boundary. It was named after the Harvey family, prominent in the 18th century for wool, banking, trade and military men in the City, and who provided the city with eight mayors and seven sheriffs. As late as 1840 Harvey Lane was known as Rose's Lane after the Rose family who had owned land locally; it was adopted in 1902.

Crinkle-crankle wall in Harvey Lane

Heartsease Lane

The Heartsease is the wild pansy (from the French word 'pensee') once common in the area.

Heathside Road

This denotes the road between two beauty spots, namely Mousehold Heath and the Wensum Valley.

High Green

Assumed to be named after the bowling green formerly on the site.

Hilary Avenue

Named after a member of the family of builders 'Grange and Samuels' who developed the area.

Hill House Road

Hill House is a listed building built around 1840.

Holmwood Rise

Named by the developer in 1980, after Holmwood House by the Harvey family.

Looking down Hill House Road across the Wensum valley

Honey Close

Charles William Honey served as a Governor of Norwich Prison from November 1952 to July 1956.

- K -

Kerrison Road

Sir Roger Kerrison was Sheriff in 1774 and Mayor in 1778 and 1802. He was a Banker with premises in the Back of the Inns, now known as Castle House.

Ketts Hill

This was once known as Strowte Hill, (meaning straight, hard and difficult). In 1549 Robert Kett headed a serious uprising as a result of the enclosure of common land and other matters. He and thousands of followers gathered on what is now the open space known as Kett's Heights, to the south of Ketts Hill. The Kett brothers were hanged, Robert at Norwich Castle and his brother William at Wymondham.

Knox Avenue, Knox Close, Knox Road

In 1930 the name of Knox Road was changed from Prison Road to commemorate a former Prison Commissioner. Knox Avenue and Knox Close are more recent developments.

Koblenz Avenue

Named after one of Norwich's twin cities, Koblenz in Germany. The formal twinning took place on 22nd April 1978 in Koblenz. Koblenz Avenue is a new road created as part of the Riverside redevelopment of the 1990s.

- L -

Ladbrooke Place

Named after John Berney Ladbrooke, artist of the Norwich School and a drawing master. He built his house 'Kett's Castle Villa' in nearby St. Leonard's Road in the late 1850s. His initials are to be seen in the brickwork of a chimney-stack there. He died in 1879 and is buried in Rosary Cemetery.

Lionwood Road

Named after the adjacent wood. The street name signs at either end of the road differ as to the spelling: "Lionwood" or "Lion Wood".

Lloyd Road

Assumed to be named after Lloyd Samuels son of one of the builders involved.

Lollards Road

The Lollards were a body of reformers under Wycliffe subjected to much persecution in the reign of Richard II. A revival of Lollardism in 1500 resulted in the Norwich executions, with a number of them being burned to death at a pit near here, so located because it was outside the city walls. A plaque near the river commemorates some of the martyrs.

Lower Clarence Road

As for Clarence Road, named after the sailor prince, subsequently William IV, in anticipation of a harbour that was never built.

- M -

Malvern Road

Meaning 'a bare hill' as in the watering place of Malvern and the hills near there.

Marion Road

Marion was a daughter of the developer Isaac Bugg Coaks. This road was one of the six 'Lady' roads. See also Beatrice, Ella, Ethel, Florence and Primrose Roads.

Matlock Road

Perhaps to recall a pleasant holiday in the Derbyshire town of that name - no other information available.

Marion Road

Mons Avenue

Named in memory of the Battle of Mons fought on 23rd August 1914 between the British Expeditionary Force of 65,000 and the 1st German Army of 160,000. The medal, the 'Mons Star', was awarded to troops serving between 5th August and 23rd November.

Montcalm Road

This road was not adopted until 1975. It was named after the French General in command of the French forces in Canada, where he was defeated and killed in 1759. See also Quebec and Wolfe Roads.

Morse Avenue, Morse Road

Named after Sir George Morse of Beech Hill, Thorpe St. Andrew. He served on Norwich Council for 34 years, was Mayor in 1898 and Lord Mayor from 1922 to 1923, the year in which he was knighted. He was also a principal of Steward and Patteson's Brewery.

Mossfield Close

This is thought to be named after the developer Joseph Moss. It is referred to in a Highways Committee meeting of 13th September 1965.

- N -

Newbegin Road, Newbegin Close

Named after a city Mayor in 1403, or possibly after Mr G. Newbegin, a keen astronomer, who lived in Thorpe-next-Norwich in the late 19th century. He resided at Town House, where he built his observatory, a familiar landmark at the time.

- O -

Oak Lodge

A mansion of this name was built on Harvey Land in 1877; a large oak tree still stands on the corner of Thorpe Road and Harvey Lane.

Old Library Mews

A branch of the County Library was on this site, which was also formerly County Council offices.

- P -

Pilling Park Road

A road adjacent to Pilling Park. The Park was presented to the City by Mrs Joseph Pilling in memory of her father Jeremiah Woodrow, a Freeman of Norwich city, and it was opened on 29th June 1929. For a number of years it was known as Woodrow Pilling Park. The name is also given to the surrounding estate, developed by Norwich City Council after it purchased the Mousehold House estate in the 1930s.

Pilling Park

Plumstead Road

The road towards Great and Little Plumstead, where plum trees grew.

Primrose Road

Primrose was a daughter of the developer Isaac Bugg Coaks. This road was one of the six 'Lady' roads. See also Beatrice, Ella, Ethel, Florence and Primrose Roads.

Providence Place

This is a common road name. Some years ago when life was cheap and expectations much less than nowadays, the belief in 'Providence' was much more widespread. The area now known as Providence Place was redeveloped in the late 1960s.

- Q -

Quebec Road

Adopted by the Corporation in 1899, and named after the Canadian city of Quebec and the battle between the Generals Wolfe and Montcalm (British and French respectively) both of whom died in the battle. The road was built approximately 140 years after the battle. See also Montcalm and Wolfe Roads.

- R -

Ranson Road

Named after Joshua Farrar Ranson, a very popular Norwich Timber Merchant. He was Sheriff in 1883 and then Mayor of the City in 1888/89; he lived in Heathside House.

Riseway Close

No information available.

Riverside

Prior to the redevelopment of the Riverside area in the 1990s the road ran alongside the river to Carrow Bridge.

Riverside Road

In 1890 Norwich Town Council entered into a contract with Mr R. A. Cooper for the purchase of land in Thorpe Hamlet required for the construction of a road adjacent to the River Wensum. The road runs north from Foundry Bridge to a junction with Rosary Road just south of Bishop Bridge. It used to be a route from trams, extending in the summer onto Mousehold Heath.

Tram on Riverside Road

Rosary Road

This was once called Chalk Hill Road. It was named after the Rosary Cemetery, the first non-denominational cemetery in the country, founded by the Rev. Thomas Drummond in 1819. Before the construction of Foundry Bridge this was the road to Great Yarmouth, as it left Norwich by Bishop Bridge, then the only bridge on that side of the city centre.

Rosedale Crescent

Said to be named after a rose garden on the site.

Roseville Close

No information available.

- S -

St. Leonard's Road

Named after St. Leonard's Priory. Bishop Herbert Losinga, the founder of Norwich Cathedral, built the church and the Priory of St Leonard's after he acquired, by charter from Henry I, the manor of Thorpe and Thorpe Wood. The priory land was on the west side of St. Leonard's Road from Gas Hill down almost to Rosary Road. A section of wall that may have once been part of the priory wall can be seen opposite the junction with Marion Road. St Leonard is the patron saint of of political prisoners, imprisoned people, prisoners of war, and captives, women in labour, as well as horses.

Old wall in St. Leonard's Road

St. Matthew's Road

Previously known as Kissing Alley, a local lovers name. The name was changed when St. Matthew's was built in the mid-19th century. The present-day St. Matthew's is in Telegraph Lane West, the former church now being used for offices..

Salisbury Road

No information available.

Samuel Road

Thought to be named by the developer of the area - Grange and Samuels, or alternatively after Mr Arthur N. Samuel, Lord Mayor in 1913, who was both 'rich' and 'free' with his money.

Sandholme Close

No information available.

Saunders Court

Formerly Bakers' Road, from the public house there, and prior to that Losinga Road, after the first Bishop of Norwich.

Scott Road

Named after the Director of Laurence Scott and Electromotors. Scott Road is part of the Thorpe Park estate, built on the site of a former Laurence Scott factory. See also Glendenning and Wilson Roads.

Sienna Mews

No information available.

Worker in the Laurence Scott factory

Spitalfields

The Great Hospital owned much of the land around here, and the term 'Spittle'or 'Spittal' denotes dwellers or attendants in a hospital. It existed as a highway as far back as 1830.

Stanley Avenue

Edward Stanley was Bishop of Norwich for 12 years. He was born in 1799 and buried in the nave of Norwich Cathedral on 21st September 1849.

Stan Petersen Close

Stan Petersen represented Thorpe Hamlet as Labour councillor on the City Council and also for four years on the County Council. He served as Deputy Lord Mayor and then as Lord Mayor in 1984. The Crome Centre, which was once a boy's school, and later a recreational centre run by the City Council, and attached to Stuart School for girls stood on the site of what is now Stan Petersen Close. From its inception as a recreational centre, Stan Petersen was a member of the committee which was responsible for the Crome Centre, and ultimately became Chairman of the committee. After the demolition of the building the City Council agreed that the road should be named after Stan Petersen as a tribute for all his work for both the city and the Crome Centre.

Station Approach

This is the road leading up to Norwich Thorpe Station from Koblenz Avenue.

Steepgreen Close

Assumed to be a reference to its steep incline.

Stracey Road

In 1868 Sir Henry Stracey was returned as Member of Parliament for Norwich. His family were noted as being among the Norfolk Gentry for many years. The road follows the line of the old carriage way from Thorpe Road to Stracey House.

Supple Close

The Reverend W. R. Supple was Rector of Thorpe-next-Norwich in the early 20th century. In 1917 an oak lectern was presented to the church in memory of the Rector's wife.

- T -

Telegraph Lane East, Telegraph Lane West

In the early 19th century a line of signalling stations was erected from Great Yarmouth to the Admiralty in London. This was at the time of the Napoleonic wars. There were 19 stations between Great Yarmouth and London and one of the stations was on the site in Telegraph Lane where the water tower and resrvoirs now stand, and which is probably the highest point in Norwich. A message could be relayed between Great Yamouth and London in less than 30 minutes, weather permitting.

The cathedral viewed through the water tower on Telegraph Lane East

The Nest

Named after the former use of this site as part of the Norwich City Club football ground prior to the move to Carrow Road in the 1930s. See also Bertram Way.

The Ridgeway

No information available.

The Sidings

This new development off Cremorne Lane adjoins the railway line from Norwich station towards Cromer and Yarmouth.

Thorpe Road

This is the road that leads from the city to Thorpe-by-Norwich, described in 1810 as a beautiful village on the north side of the river, containing many houses delightfully situated. It was part of the Great Yarmouth turnpike road. The road from Foundry Bridge to the corner of Rosary Road was once called 'Foundry Bridge Road'.

Timothy Close

No information available.

- V -

Valley Side Road

Named for its physical features.

Venables Close

No information available.

Vincent Road

VE and VJ party in Vincent Road, August 1945

Believed to have been named in honour of George Vincent (1796-1831), a respected member of the Norwich School of painters; he was, in fact, a pupil of John Crome. See also Cotman Road and Ladbrooke Place.

- W -

Wellesley Avenue North, Wellesley Avenue South

Wellesley Avenue South

Built on land formerly owned by Sir Robert Harvey, of Mousehold House. The road was named after Arthur Wellesley, later known as the Duke of Wellington, and younger son of the First Earl of Mornington. He was born in Dublin on 1st May 1769. He later became Prime Minister. He died in 1852. Colonel Sir Robert Harvey fought with the Duke of Wellington in Portugal in the Peninsula Wars. Harvey also helped the son of the Duke to become MP for Norwich. See also Cintra Road and William Mear Gardens.

Wherry Road

A wherry is a type of boat used on the rivers and broads of Norfolk and Suffolk. Most were trading vessels but some were built as pleasure boats. See also Albion Way.

Whitwell Road

Whitwell means the 'white spring' or stream. The word goes back to Saxon days. There is also a Norfolk village of this name.

William Kett Close

William was the brother of Robert Kett. See Ketts Hill.

William Mear Gardens

William Mear, a local architect, was the designer used by Sir Robert Harvey when he remodelled Mousehold House. He also laid out the surrounding grounds.

Mousehold House in William Mear Gardens

William White Place

William White was one of the Lollards of Ludham. He was brought before Bishop Alnwick and condemned to be burnt at the area near Bishop Bridge which is called Lollards' Pit. He died in 1428. See also Lollards Road.

Wilson Road

No information available about the choice of name. Wilson Road is part of the Thorpe Park estate, built on the site of a former Laurence Scott factory. See also Glendenning and Scott Roads.

Wolfe Road

James Wolfe was a British general from 1727 to 1759. (This road was adopted in 1899). After being killed on the Plains of Abraham in Quebec, he was buried in Greenwich. See also Montcalm and Quebec Roads,

Womersley Close, Womersley Road

Joseph Womersley, who died in March 1899, worked for J. and J. Colman, and was practically the founder of the rice-starch industry.

Woodrow Place

Named after Jeremiah Woodrow, father of Mrs Joseph Pilling of Manchester, who donated Pilling Park in honour of her father who formerly lived in Norwich. Jeremiah became a Freeman of the City in 1826. He left Norwich in 1829 to set up his company J. Woodrow and Son, hat manufacturers in Stockport. He always retained a great interest in Norwich where he still had family connections. See also Pilling Park Road.

INDEX TO STREETS SHOWN ON THE MAP

Albert Place............................B5
Albion Way.............................A7
Aldryche Road.....................D3
Aspland Road.....................A6

Barrack Road........................C4
Barton Way........................C7
Beatrice Road.................B5, B6
Belsize Road.........................C4
Bertram Way......................B5
Bishop Bridge Road.......B4, B5
Borrowdale Drive...D2, D3, E2
Britannia Road.........B3, C3, C4
Broadsman Close...........B7, B8

Camp Grove.........................C5
Canary Way....................B7, B8
Carrow Road............B7, B8, C7
Cedar Road..........................C7
Chalk Hill Road.............A6, B6
Cintra Road..................C6, D6
Clarence Road.....................C7
Cotman Road.........C6, C7, D6
Cozens Road...................B8, C8
Cremorne Lane....................D7
Croftholme Way..................E2
Cubitt Road..................D4, E4

Dugard Avenue...................D2

Eden Close............................E6
Ella Road..............................B6
Ethel Road............................B6

Fallowfield Close...........D2, E2
Fernhill Lane..................C6, C7
Ferry Road............................A5
Firwood Close.....................E2
Florence Road......................B6

Gas Hill...................................B5
Geoffrey Watling Way.........B8
Gerald Close..................D2, E2
Glendenning Road..............D7
Gravelfield Close.................D2
Guelph Road.......................B5
Gurney Road............................
..............B2, B3, B4, C1, C2, D1
Harbour Road......................C7
Hardy Road...................C7, C8
Harvey Lane.......E3, E4, E5, E6

Heartsease Lane D1, E1, E2, E3
Heathside Road..............C6, C7
High Green...........................C6
Hilary Avenue..............D3, D4
Hill House Road...................B6
Holmwood Rise...................E5
Honey Close..................C3, D3

Kerrison Road.................B8, C8
Ketts Hill.......................B4, C4
Knox Avenue................C3, D3
Knox Close....................C3, D3
Knox Road...............C3, C4, D4
Koblenz Avenue............A7, B7

Ladbrooke Place...................B4
Lionwood Road....................D4
Lloyd Road...........................D3
Lollards Road.................A5, B5
Lower Clarence Rd..A6, B6, B7

Malvern Road.......................B5
Marion Road.........................B6
Matlock Road.......................D7
Mons Avenue.................B2, B3
Montcalm Road....................C5
Morse Avenue......................E4
Morse Road...........................E4
Mossfield Close..............C2, C3

Newbegin Close.............D4, E4
Newbegin Road....................D4

Oak Lodge.............................E6
Old Library Mews................B6

Pilling Park Road....D4, D5, E4
Plumstead Rd...C4, D3, D4, E3
Primrose Road...............B5, C5
Providence Place..................C5

Quebec Road............B4, C4, C5

Ranson Road.........................D6
Riseway Close.......................D3
Riverside........................A6, B7
Riverside Road........A5, A6, B5
Rosary Road...................B5, B6
Rosedale Crescent................B6
Roseville Close.....................D7

St. Leonard's Rd.B4, B5, B6, C5
St. Matthew's Road........A6, B6
Salisbury Road.....................D7
Samuel Road.........................D3
Sandholme Close..................C2
Saunders Court....................B5
Scott Road.....................C7, D7
Sienna Mews.........................D4
Spitalfields............................B4
Stanley Avenue....................E6
Stan Petersen Close..............C6
Station Approach.................A6
Steepgreen Close............D3, E3
Stracey Road..................B6, B7
Supple Close...................E3, E4

Telegraph Lane E... C5, C6, D6
Telegraph Lane West.... B5, C5
The Nest.................................B5
The Ridgeway.................D2,D3
The Sidings...........................D7
Thorpe Road............................
........A6, B6, B7, C7, D6, D7, E7
Timothy Close......................D3

Valley Side Road............D3, E3
Venables Close................C4,D4
Vincent Road........................C4

Wellesley Avenue Nth. D4, D5
Wellesley Avenue South.....D6
Wherry Road.................A7, A8
Whitwell Road......................B4
William Kett Close...............B5
William Mear Gardens........D5
William White Place.............B5
Wilson Road.........................C7
Wolfe Road.............C4, C5, D5
Womersley Close.................D4
Womersley Road..................D4
Woodrow Place.....................D5

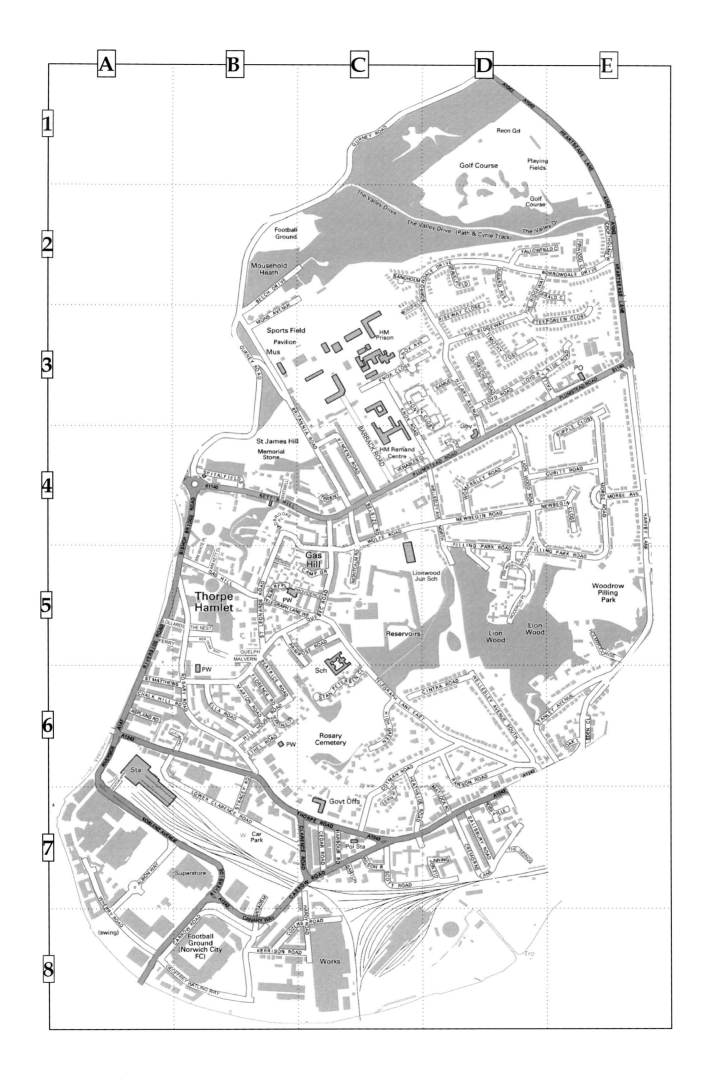